BOWIE: HIS STYLE PRINCIPLES

Natalie
Hammond

BOWIE

HIS STYLE PRINCIPLES

BE INSPIRED, DRESS OUT OF THIS WORLD

POP PRESS

CONTENTS

INTRODUCTION

'An outfit is much
more than just
something to wear
– it's about who you
are; it's a badge, it
becomes a symbol.'

DAVID BOWIE

David Bowie's clothes were as much of a trademark as those mismatched pupils, as crucial a part of the man's mythology as his electrified red hair. But here's the curious thing: he wasn't actually interested in fashion. This was the man who wore dresses, capes and a one-legged bodysuit with flames 'licking' his crotch as his androgynous alien pin-up, Ziggy Stardust. The man who made it cool to look a little bit like you were from outer space. He broke so many boundaries over his five decades on stage. And he did it just as much with what he wore as with his ever-shifting sound.

Isn't Bowie not being interested in fashion a bit like Elvis Presley, who was born on exactly the same date 12 years earlier, not being interested in sideburns or flared jumpsuits? Not exactly. Bowie certainly used fashion to his advantage – he had an exceptional understanding of clothing's transformative effect. It's just that being fashionable in itself was never part of his manifesto.

'The thing is, I always wore clothes for a reason, not to be fashionable. I've never seen the point in being fashionable, as then you obviously just look like everyone else', he explained in an interview with journalist and author Dylan Jones, as documented in *David Bowie: A Life*. Bowie didn't want to follow trends. He didn't even particularly want to set them. Instead, he wanted to be them, defining an era's mood with a hairstyle or the cut of a suit. 'It doesn't matter in what context you're talking about, I never ever wanted to be, or look remotely like, anyone else.'

In his early years of success in the seventies, Bowie also didn't want to be himself onstage. David Jones, the boy from the 'burbs who'd come of age in Brixton, Bromley and Beckenham wasn't who he gave to the public. Instead, he constructed a series of identities, stepping into the shoes of Major Tom, Ziggy Stardust, Aladdin Sane and the Thin White Duke, using costumes, make-up and hair dye rather like an actor. It wasn't real, but a performance, a continual act of metamorphosis to avoid clinging to the past. Bowie was always the present and the future, whether he was wearing a kimono or a white T-shirt.

He might not have been preoccupied with fashion, once quipping that all one needed was a 'clean pair of shoes' during an interview for *Bust Magazine*, but, boy, did he have style. And that was something quite different entirely. In a profile with *Complex*, which was part of a conversation with hip hop artist and actor Mos Def, Bowie said that the two were almost mutually exclusive terms. 'Ironically, style doesn't even come closely related to fashion,' he said. 'Style is about the choices you make to create the aspects of civilization that you wish to uphold.' He went on to explain that you don't buy a chair because of how it looks. You buy it because the height of its seat, the curve of its back or the style of its legs, for example, say something about you. (I would have loved to have seen what was around his dining table.)

That's ultimately one of the most important style principles you can learn from Bowie. It's not about whether this silhouette is 'in' or 'out'. It's more an expression of selfhood. And if that sounds esoteric, it simply means you should wear what feels right to you, whether or not it's strictly on trend. In fact, Bowie didn't have a modus operandi. He wore eye-poppingly bold colour combinations, then black and white. His silhouettes were slim-fit one minute and supersized the next. Even his sandy blond hair was a blank canvas for experimentation.

Each chapter of this book will walk you through a principle of Bowie's, explaining how to use some of his most famous looks as a springboard for your own creativity when it comes to getting dressed. If you take only one thing away from reading this book, it should be the following: do not be afraid to rip up the rulebook, to be a contradiction, to be a bit more Bowie.

CHOOSE

BO
LD

COLOURS

Bowie didn't always get it right when it came to colour. In an interview with *Rolling Stone*'s Kurt Loder, he talks candidly about his early fashion forays as part of The Konrads. 'We wore gold corduroy jackets, I remember, and brown mohair trousers and green, brown, and white ties, I think, and white shirts. Strange coloration.' Indeed. But that all changed with Ziggy Stardust.

In Dylan Jones' biography *David Bowie: A Life*, a rich and remarkable oral history told through contributions from more than 180 interviewees, the author remembers what it was like watching him perform on *Top of the Pops*. Appearing like some sort of messiah in living rooms up and down the country, Bowie was wearing a quilted suit that clung rather sexily to his limbs, made by his tailor at the time, Freddie Burretti. This was 1972 and it was like the second coming. Ziggy Stardust was the new rock god – and he was dressed in gold, red and blue. At one point

'We were all bright
rainbow colours,
glittering, sparkling,

and they were in denim.'

WOODY WOODMANSEY

during a remastered clip of *Starman*, he looks down his nose into the camera and points, wiggling his finger straight at you. It's hard to describe how life-altering it was as a viewing experience, although Jones manages to sum it up quite succinctly: 'For me, he kick-started the seventies, as the decade turned from black and white to colour overnight.'

Bowie inspired a whole generation of teenagers to go red, dyeing their hair with presumably whatever they could find at the local chemist to make it sufficiently flame-like. He was alive with colour, from his head to his feet, which were also as red as an anthurium thanks to his platform boots. When Bowie stepped into those shoes – or was helped into them owing to their considerable height – he became a different character, a prophet from another planet whose costumes would change before his audience's eyes. The colours were a part and parcel of the magic.

If you watch clips of his last appearance as Ziggy, at his infamous concert at the

Hammersmith Odeon, you can see these rapid-fire changes in action. As Bowie starts *Ziggy Stardust*, he's wearing a black diamond-shaped jumpsuit with shots of blue and red, his feet planted about a metre apart. Two pairs of hands materialise out of the darkness and deftly yank its sleeves, revealing the famously short white satin kimono, which is positively luminescent under the stage lights. He does the same thing again later with two more outfits by Kansai Yamamoto: the white cape revealing the marvellous, multi-coloured jumpsuit. At one point, Bowie goes offstage to change into his sculpted-shoulder two-piece, another number by Burretti, which he wears with the boots. You can tell how tight it is, because he grimaces as it goes up his legs. He smooths out each of his sleeves so that they sit just so. He must have looked something like a red, blue and silver mirage, a sensory assault on your eyes and ears that made them explode with colour and sound. Exhilarating doesn't even begin to describe it. This was nothing short of earth-shattering.

FINDING YOUR CONFIDENCE COLOUR

The first thing to note is that confidence colours don't translate as bold colours to everyone. Some feel most like themselves in a spectrum of black, navy and charcoal. There's nothing wrong with that at all. I know plenty of people who stick to a similar rotation, occasionally introducing biscuit or cream to break it up. But for the purposes of this chapter, why not do what you do best while pushing the boundaries at the same time? A fresh take on colour-blocking that encompasses three neutrals but mixes in something more statement is grey, black, white and fire-engine red. I would wear the combination as follows (give or take a little, of course, depending on what you have in your wardrobe): a grey coat, black court heels and trousers, white shoulder bag and red polo neck. You only need a dash of colour to create an impact. Of course, a similar effect could be achieved with a swipe of lipstick – either red or something more unusual like tangerine or violet.

Some people are completely the opposite, feeling washed out or perhaps even disempowered when they're dressed in colours that they consider drab. They're most at home when they're wearing at least one highly-pigmented shade, the kind that packs a punch. If this rings true for your approach to colour, you've probably got a good idea of what you feel happiest wearing, whether it's grapefruit orange or seafoam green.

But what if you fall somewhere in the middle, wanting to mostly blend in, but occasionally stand out? Firstly, most of us occupy this space, so you're far from alone. What you need to do is find out which colours you're naturally drawn towards – this is just as important as what suits you. This is the perfect opportunity to go window shopping, because you don't need to part with any money to see what catches your eye. A Kelly-green pair of trousers, for example, or a cherry-red jacket. Once you've set your sights on a particular colour, try to imagine what it would be like wearing it in real life, not just in a changing room. Your gut reaction to the question of whether or not you already have something in your wardrobe to wear that shade with is probably the right one.

Another way to find 'the one' is to look at the wardrobes of celebrities who you think wear colours well. Actor Tracee Ellis Ross never met a shade of yellow she couldn't make look sublime, although it has to be said that she also wears a lot of neutrals. See? I told you it wasn't all black and white.

HOW
TO

This is where it gets complicated. Because although it sounds like an obvious no, clashing colours is actually a big yes. Let me explain. Some colours are so wrong they're right. And these are usually the pairings that sit very close to each other on the colour wheel, like red and pink or black and navy. True 'complementary' colours sit opposite one another: red and green, orange and blue, yellow and purple. But although they technically suit one another, you wouldn't necessarily wear them together (the pairing of red and green, naturally, gets a free pass during the festive season).

CLASH
YOUR

COLOURS

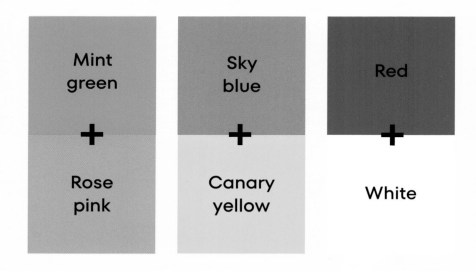

It's the slightly less obvious, slightly more 'off' duos that will pass muster with the fashion crowd. Bowie favoured yellow and black, wearing them together on a pair of striped trousers by Versace, or yellow and white, which he wore to great effect on the Low/Heroes Tour. You can either copy these tried-and-tested colour formulas, or reinvent the wheel with your own.

True aficionados will often be able to blend three or four shades together to make one seamless colour story. It's quite a sight to behold, but easier to copy than you might imagine. (Note that you'll want to try this style manoeuvre

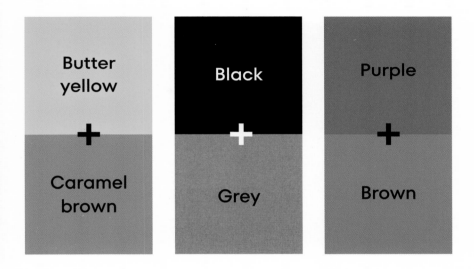

using solid colours. Introducing a print is a step too far if this is your first time.) As mentioned earlier, grey, black, white and red go particularly well together. But if we just take two – white and red – you can have all kinds of fun with shades from sky blue, to rose pink, to mint green, to butter yellow.

Bowie threw caution to the wind when it came to wearing colour, pairing green with black, white and gold – and that was before you factored in his hair. So really, the only rule is that there are no rules.

RED RULES

Despite wearing many different colours, Bowie's Ziggy persona has become synonymous with red for two reasons: his hair and his boots. It's also a colour that has never fallen out of fashion. Bowie very memorably wore it from top-to-toe during 1987's Glass Spider Tour.

At its most primary, post-box red can be powerful and sexy, whether you're fully immersed or merely wearing a flash. Even looping a red handbag over your shoulder manages to convey a kind of confidence that you just can't achieve with tan. (You can create a similar effect with red footwear, using a vermillion gloved pump as a punctuation mark at the end of your outfit.) A deeper red like burgundy, carmine or wine, meanwhile, is an even more grown-up way to wear the colour, making every shade that sits next to it look richer.

In turns of which shade to wear when, I've always subscribed to the belief that summer calls for a charged approach to the colour. Chilli-pepper red really suits satin, so a slip dress is your best bet – and as such a perennial style on the high street, you'll have no shortage of affordable options if you don't already have one hanging in your wardrobe. By autumn, I find myself drawn towards red-wine hues, which work brilliantly with heavier-gauge fabrics like wool or corduroy. You can switch things up, of course. A claret-coloured lip can be a nice change of pace in the warmer months, while a shock of scarlet can lift the spirits in the bleak mid-winter period.

'BOWIE' COLOUR

Ziggy was one of Bowie's only characters who wore a rainbow of colours – from aqua, to silver, to red – and that was just for *Life on Mars?* His others stuck quite closely to two or three shades. The Thin White Duke was a monochrome man, as was Bowie's last incarnation, The Blind Prophet. His *Let's Dance* era, on the other hand, was categorised by a pastel palette of all things: a full-fat selection of ice cream shades that cut a strangely dashing contrast with his bottle-blond hair. The following list isn't exhaustive, but is more of a rough guide to which colours he wore as which character. What it absolutely does do, though, is give you an accurate impression of the man's willingness to experiment, wearing shades that were dreamily soft, then sharply acidic. Of course, he looked brilliant in them all.

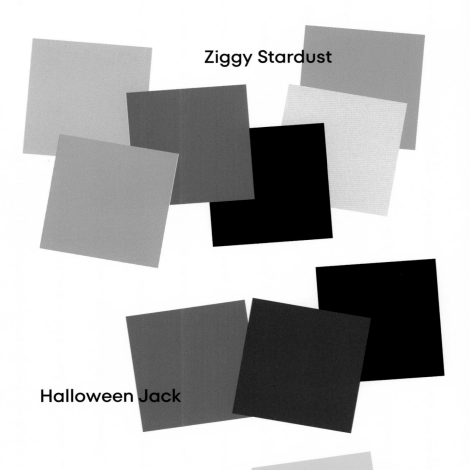

Ziggy Stardust

Halloween Jack

The Soul Man

Thin White Duke

The DJ

Pierrot

Serious Moonlight Tour

Glass Spider Tour

Tin Machine Tour

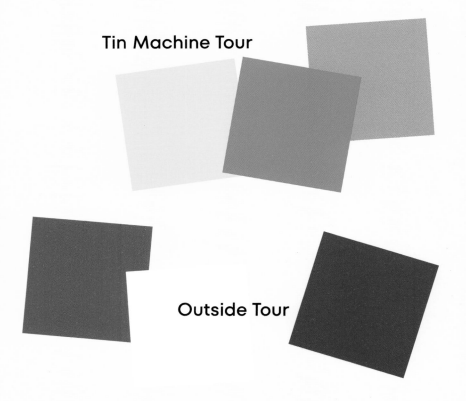

Outside Tour

PLAY

WITH

PROPORTIONS

'Wide shoulders are the flared trousers of the eighties.'

DAVID BOWIE

It was 1973. Unsuspecting fans arriving at the Hammersmith Odeon – their eyelids perhaps painted peacock blue out of a respectful mania for their alien hero – were about to receive the emotional equivalent of a one-two punch from Bowie. Not only was this his last concert on the tour, but he was killing off Ziggy Stardust. He'd inspired a generation of youngsters to play fast and loose with their hair, their make-up, their very idea of what was 'male' and what was 'female'. What on earth would be his next move?

The answer was Aladdin Sane. Although he wasn't a complete about-turn from Ziggy Stardust – they shared the same haircut, after all – his was an altogether more troubling personality. As Rob Sheffield, *Rolling Stone* journalist and lifelong fan of Bowie's, put it in his book, *On Bowie*: 'Aladdin Sane is a harder, nastier, kinkier story than Ziggy Stardust, written on the road and immersed in the sleaze of

American culture.' Aladdin Sane was a kind of postscript for Ziggy, a dark parting shot to the intoxicating glitter of glam rock.

While the two characters had a shared history of sorts, Bowie would presumably have wanted a distinct look for his latest incarnation. Kansai Yamamoto – still his right-hand man when it came to costumes that could quite easily command a stage on their own, whether or not they were being worn by David Bowie – stepped up to the plate once again, delivering an all-in-one that was the antithesis of the skin-tight silhouette of Ziggy.

The Tokyo Pop jumpsuit wasn't a piece of clothing so much as it was a voluminous optical illusion. Rendered in vinyl, its proportions were no less than extraordinary, probably measuring a couple of metres from knee to knee. People were so used to seeing every contour of Bowie – from his chest, to his bicep, to his calf – that this was a truly shocking turn of events. It also had a backstory that would have appealed, I think, to his voracious appetite for just about any interesting subject. In *The Guardian*'s obituary of Yamamoto, who died in 2020, the jumpsuit's origin story is described as, 'Oskar Schlemmer's Bauhaus ballet designs and the galligaskin breeches of Portuguese sailors and merchants trading with Japan in the 16th–17th centuries.'

It certainly wouldn't be the last time that Bowie changed the shape of his body simply with his clothes. (Actually, it wasn't even the first. On the back cover of *Hunky Dory*, he's wearing a high-waisted, loose-legged pair of trousers that were allowed to dominate the shot because of the camera's positioning.) And although this sounds like something that's part of theatre and not everyday life, it's actually something that you probably do, to a certain extent, every time you get dressed, without even realising you're doing it.

KANSAI

YAMAMOTO

Kansai Yamamoto's designs weren't just an ingredient in the making of Ziggy Stardust, they were instrumental to his genesis. The Japanese designer gave the glam-rock alien his haircut, his eyebrows (or lack thereof) and his wardrobe. In 1971, Yamamoto staged a show in London. *Harpers & Queen* called it a 'spectacular coup de theatre', presumably in praise of the 'basara' methodology behind his work. Yamamoto gave the following definition to the Victoria and Albert Museum: 'Basara means to dress freely, with a stylish extravagance.' He could have been talking about Ziggy. Bowie was already familiar with Yamamoto's work by the time they met in 1973. Bowie was actually wearing them to perform when the designer came backstage at Radio City Music Hall. The rest is history. Yamamoto went on to make some of Bowie's most famous outfits – like the pearl white cape, personalised with kanji characters that spelt out 'David Bowie', and the vinyl jumpsuit for Aladdin Sane – both of which allowed the quick costume changes used in kabuki theatre, *hikinuki*, that famously inspired Bowie.

THE
RIGHT

Yamamoto's jumpsuit is a textbook example of an enduring style principle – even the most dramatic outfit needs a sense of balance. Easy to articulate, hard to pull off, but in fact, the best pieces will do it for you. The jumpsuit is again a case in point. The bottom half might look almost inflatable, ballooning outwards to give each limb an exaggeratedly curvaceous shape, but what about the top half's turtleneck? And the slim-fit sleeves? It's the definition of perfectly proportioned.

You're probably setting your sights on something a little more subtle than that jumpsuit. Fair enough. But you still need to bear the same balancing act in mind, especially with separates. As a general rule of thumb, in order to keep your outfit in proportion, one piece needs to be a statement in terms of shape, and the other should be more of a supporting act. Say, for example, a barrel-legged jean which curves out from the knee then tapers towards the ankle (statement), with a graphic polo neck (supporting act). Now, a graphic polo neck might sound fairly statement. That's because there's often a secondary balancing act to be struck – and that's between something loud and something quiet. A barrel-legged jean might have an arresting silhouette, but it's still quite everyday. A graphic polo neck is the opposite – it is everyday in shape, but statement in personality. See the list over the page for other examples.

Don't forget your bag, which is an essential part of the balancing act. If you're wearing something either busy or baggy on top, you'll want to carry something streamlined. An unwieldy tote will weigh you down in more than just the obvious sense. Instead, pick a structured shoulder bag that will sit neatly under your armpit. Alternatively, something like a pared-back coat can take a bit of amping up when it comes to accessories. Try something leathery that's either woven, patchworked or quilted, perhaps with an interesting strap (like chain-link, for example).

The same rule applies to shoes. If your statement piece sits on your bottom half, you'll want a shoe that's a little more tame. For example, you can give a cuddly pair of wide-legged corduroy trousers some attitude with a pointed slingback pump.

BALANCE

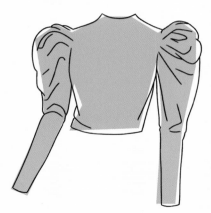

Shirt with leg-of-mutton sleeves

wool pencil skirt

Black bolero jacket

high-waisted palazzo pants

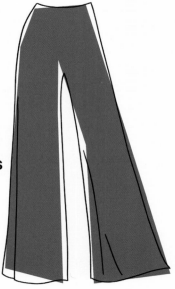

Velvet Blazer

straight-leg jeans

Crew-neck cashmere jumper
+
flaring floral skirt

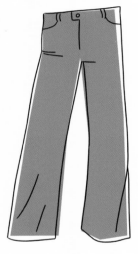

Single-breasted black coat
+
wide-legged corduroy trousers

Shearling-trimmed leather jacket
+
denim maxi skirt

OUTFIT IDEAS

The easiest way to create an interesting outline is by basing your look around one hero silhouette, whether that's a snazzily tailored blazer or a snatched-waist trouser.

Ziggy's more 'off-duty' wardrobe consisted of blazers with impressively big lapels. A modern equivalent is a tailored jacket with a sharp set of shoulders, which is guaranteed to earn its keep as a wardrobe workhorse because of its ability to be dressed up or down.

SHARP-SHOULDERED BLAZER

T-shirt	Tank top	Crew-neck cardigan	Striped shirt
+	+	+	+
Straight-legged jeans	Denim pencil skirt	Bouclé miniskirt	Stirrup leggings
+	+	+	+
Knee-high suede boot	Slingback pump	Loafer	Ballet pump

Bowie flirted with any number of trouser shapes, but was committed to the high waist all along. Once you've found your perfect fit, which might involve a trip to your local dry-cleaner to make sure it's truly nipped, there's a world of possibilities out there.

HIGH-WAISTED TROUSERS

With wide legs		With tapered legs	
Single-breasted coat	Shell bomber jacket	Shearling leather jacket	Oversized denim shirt
+	+	+	+
Cropped cardigan	T-shirt	Crew-neck jumper	Long-sleeved ribbed top
+	+	+	+
Kitten-heeled boot	Chelsea boot	Crystal-embellished flat	Suede cowboy boot

Most people have something striped in their wardrobe. In fact, I often find on work video calls that a handful of those present will start laughing as soon as the feed starts, because they're all wearing a navy-and-white Breton. Sadly, Bowie didn't do business with garden-variety stripes. Instead, he often used the pattern to create an optical illusion with his body, making the eye see things he wanted it to see. The Aladdin Sane jumpsuit, for example, isn't really striped at all. Instead, it's an expanding set of triangles that is split over the legs, torso, arms and neck.

This wasn't the only time that Bowie used a simple assembly of lines to his advantage. In May 1973, he was touring around the country in what, unbeknownst to fans, would be among his last appearances as Ziggy Stardust. Photographed at King's Cross Station, Bowie emerged onto the platform wearing a black-and-white striped blazer by his good friend, and even better tailor, Freddie Burretti. What made your vision swim ever-so-slightly when you stared at him, however, was that the lines on his lapels were diagonal, while the lines on the jacket itself were horizontal. It was kaleidoscopic, revealing something new the longer you looked.

Not all of Bowie's stripes were mind-bending to behold, but they were still rather statement-making. Almost 20 years later, on tour with his band Tin Machine, he packed a pair of very snappy trousers which had black-and-yellow stripes running down each leg. It might be maximalist to the extreme, but it's also a supremely flattering approach, because the vertical lines make your eye run from top to bottom instead of side to side, giving the effect of lengthening the body's proportions by an impressive few inches.

Still, traffic-stopping stripes might not be everyone's cup of tea. You can't go wrong, however, with pinstripes, which, as their name would suggest, are sometimes barely perceptible. A white-on-navy stripe is the most common variety for trousers – which won't look corporate if you choose an off-beat shoe like a studded leather clog – and you can find well-tailored wool-blend styles with double-front pleats on the high street.

High street brands for expensive-looking pinstripes:

★ **H&M**

★ **Marks & Spencer**

★ **Warehouse**

★ **Weekday**

A ticking stripe shirt dress is another way to do vertical stripes. I prefer styles without a waist belt so that it's quite literally straight up and down. Palmer//Harding has a brilliant way with stripes, and shirt dresses for that matter. Season on season, you're guaranteed to find a new interpretation of each. And while we're on the subject, Issey Miyake's Pleats Please range has a pleasantly stripy effect thanks to its plissé fabrication.

Despite my love for the vertical, I don't mean to disparage horizontal stripes; they're a staple of so many wardrobes for a reason. If you do want to mix it up, there's an easy way to play with proportions – and it simply involves looking for pieces that incorporate two varieties of stripe. They don't even have to go in opposite directions to look directional. I've seen cardigans where the stripe's thickness varies on each arm, as well as polo neck jumpers with graduated stripes that thicken as they move down the torso.

In fact, Yamamoto has a tip for us here. In a black-and-white photograph from one of his fittings with Bowie, he's actually wearing a jumper version of the famous knitted jumpsuit, its geometric lines zigging across his chest as he holds a bangle aloft in his hand. It's not quite as head-turning as Aladdin Sane, but we can't all be David Bowie, can we?

PATTERN PLAY

It wasn't all about stripes. Bowie wore plenty of other patterns, once again using their proportions to his advantage.

POLKA DOTS

You might think polka dots are too conventional for someone like Bowie, but they cropped up several times throughout his career. One of the most notable examples was while Bowie was touring for *Diamond Dogs*. Ziggy was recent history, his signature hair still orange but significantly less electrified, and his new wardrobe consisted of soaringly high trousers, two-tone shoes, checked neckties – and a shrunken polka dot sweater. Its tiny spots gave the trousers even more of a sky-high quality. You can create a similar effect today by pairing a polka-dot sweater with peg-leg trousers, letting them taper off at the ankle bone instead of trailing to the floor.

FLORALS

For his last performance at Glastonbury in 2000, Bowie belted out his greatest hits, despite a recent bout of laryngitis, while wearing a kind of period costume by Alexander McQueen. His *Hunky Dory* wavy hair matched the flower vines on his gold frock coat, proving beyond a reasonable doubt that a wallpaper print can 100 per cent be rock 'n' roll. Look closely at pictures from the night in question and you'll see that he wore a long, striped shirt underneath, creating one of his most celebrated print clashes of all time. It's the best way to wear florals.

'BAROCCO'

Versace's 'Barocco' print found a fan in David Bowie, who wore one of the brand's black-and-gold bomber jackets on tour in 1991. It was casual, cool and just a little showy, cutting a wild contrast with his straight-legged jeans (not to mention with the block-coloured jackets that he had otherwise packed in his suitcases). The Italian fashion house still carries a version of the same bomber – it's now made of silk – and you can also find pre-loved versions on platforms like Vestiaire Collective.

CHECKS

Despite being someone so naturally anti-mainstream, Bowie could still look incredibly suave. There's a fabulous picture where he looks like he's just emerged from a swim at a country club – wearing white jeans, a checked jacket and a tawny tan. Of course, there was something slightly cool, slightly 'off' about the whole ensemble, as Bowie was also wearing a checked shirt with bigger squares than those on the blazer. It was another optical illusion, albeit of a more wearable kind – and you could pull exactly the same trick with any pattern.

EMBRACE THE

'At home, he usually wore jeans and a T-shirt, but when he went out, he dressed up like a prince!'

DANA GILLESPIE

Bowie didn't do boring. His restless imagination simply didn't allow him to rest on his laurels when it came to his sound or his style. It was a case of constantly ripping up the rule book, which he had probably written in the first place, and starting again with nothing, not even a lyric or a pair of trousers. But he didn't just want to be something new. He wanted to be something better. When it came to image, he played a constant game of one-upmanship – with himself. He never ran out of energy or lost the desire for something less than thrilling.

It was remarkable to witness. Just when you thought you'd seen it all after an episode involving an ostrich-feather breastplate and lace-up boots, Bowie found a whole new level of kink with a sailor's cap and stupendously high trousers. That was just how he operated, with the attitude of, 'You ain't seen nothing yet.'

That's not to say he didn't wear things twice.
If he found something sufficiently exuberant,
he would wear it not once, not twice, but three
times, without batting so much as a kohl-
rimmed eyelid. Well, so would you if you owned
a piece of history from Alexander McQueen.

Journalist Dana Thomas recalled the anecdote
in an article for *Vanity Fair*. McQueen wasn't a
household name in 1996. Bowie, however, had
heard of him. (He had an insatiable appetite
for learning about what people were reading,
watching and, probably, wearing, as well as
where they were eating, drinking and dancing.
He always made it his point to be in the know.)
He simply rang up the studio one day, letting his
assistant dictate his measurements down the
phone. McQueen was already white-hot and
soon to be hotter following his appointment to
Givenchy. Ruti Danan, his assistant at the time,
recalled that he wasn't 'impressed by
celebrities'. He nevertheless agreed to make

some stage outfits for Bowie. The Union Jack coat was purposefully distressed so that it almost looked like it was from another time. Danan remembers roughing it up in the garden with stones. It was so Bowie. I can only imagine how he must have grinned when he tried it on for the first time. Of course, it looked fabulous on stage, making Bowie look, quite literally, like rock 'n' roll royalty.

ALEXANDER MCQUEEN

The British fashion landscape would be very dull indeed without Lee Alexander McQueen. His Savile Row training gave him an impeccable flair for tailoring, while his iconoclastic design spirit led to pieces of clothing that were genuinely the first of their kind, as seen with the notorious 'bumster' trousers. Like Bowie, he had a prodigious work ethic, at one point working as creative director for Givenchy, as well as helming his eponymous label. McQueen also invented the 'viral' catwalk moment, before such a thing was technically possible, by spray-painting a model with a pair of robots for his spring/summer 1999 show. He designed several stage outfits for Bowie – and was even interviewed by the man himself over the phone for *Dazed & Confused* – but they never actually met in person. Both were the subject of blockbuster retrospectives at the Victoria and Albert Museum (Bowie in 2013; McQueen in 2015). McQueen took his own life in 2010.

A TIMELINE OF EXUBERANCE

Bowie differentiated between the rock star's onstage life versus offstage, as well as being hyper-aware that his persona when he was switched 'on' wasn't who he really was when he was 'off'. That must have been one of the reasons why his costumes – which differed from his everyday clothes quite considerably – were so exuberant, so statement-making. They were a public-facing projection of who he was at the time of that interview or that performance (or, more accurately, who he wanted you to believe he was). Of course, even as himself – Jones instead of Bowie – he'd often venture into exuberant territory, wearing a paisley waistcoat with pearl grey trousers on the red carpet, his hair slightly orange and standing on end. One thing's for certain, his style – like his ever-changing sound – kept you on your toes.

Hands

Natasha Korniloff's cobweb unitard would have been exuberant enough without the addition of stuffed gold hands that 'grabbed' at strategic body parts. Interestingly, Beyoncé wore something similarly surreal on her blockbuster Renaissance World Tour – a rhinestone-studded bodysuit by Loewe, with hands that 'clasped' at the bust and crotch.

Feathers

Bowie's 'Angel of Death' costume was a heart-shaped breastplate made of black feathers, a red latex bodysuit and thigh-high boots that had to be painstakingly laced all the way up the leg. He wore it for his famous duet with Marianne Faithfull, who was wearing a kind of nun's habit, lending the whole moment even more of a naughty-but-nice thrill.

Pierrot

Photographer Brian Duffy captured the singer made up as Pierrot, a character that he created for the cover of *Ashes to Ashes*. After Duffy had shot the full costume – another museum-worthy design by Korniloff – Bowie peeled off the suit and smoked a cigarette, revealing the tell-tale white line of make-up that stopped as his neck met his shoulders. It wasn't real, but it did make a statement.

Trousers

The sailor trousers that Bowie wore while touring in 1978 weren't a statement because of their shade, but because of their silhouette. Sometimes the art of concealing can be just as provocative as the art of revealing. These trousers were impressively high-waisted and barrel-legged, creating the illusion of hips where there weren't any. It showed a different side to Bowie, which was a statement in itself, of course.

Union Jack

The Union Jack coat signalled the meeting of two great masters in making a statement: Bowie and McQueen. It had a thoroughly punk sensibility but was also partly a relic from another time, with its high collar, padded shoulders and full 'skirt'. Wearing it on the cover of *Earthling*, Bowie faced away from the camera, looking out over a pastoral landscape that was, presumably, somewhere in Great Britain.

MAXI-MALISM

An important part of embracing the exuberant is knowing when to do exactly the opposite. Just look at the cover of *Earthling*. Bowie's Alexander McQueen coat is allowed to take centre stage, worn with black trousers that don't compete for attention so much as focus your eye on his red, white and blue regalia. Basically, if your coat's registering as a 10, you want everything else to be a three or below.

You probably know whether you're more of an introvert or an extrovert when it comes to getting dressed. (If you aren't sure, do you tend to subscribe to a 'less is more' or a 'more is more' school of thought? To put it another way, if presented with a simple cashmere cardigan, would you rather pair it with grey wool slacks or leopard-print trousers? There's your answer in a nutshell.) But I'd actually argue that no one is 100 per cent a minimalist or maximalist. You might lean more heavily towards one or the other, but the best outfits tend to incorporate elements of both.

A good starting point is to pick one statement piece. This is where your sense of minimalism or maximalism can come into play, because 'statement' will mean sequinned kick flares to one person and a slightly louder shirt than usual to another. Once you've made your choice, you can start building your outfit around it. Say you did opt for sequinned kick flares – I would dial them right down with a knitted twinset and trainers. Keep your jewellery to an everyday pair of hoop earrings so that everything but the trousers remains in soft-focus. Now, since the slightly louder shirt will cause significantly less of a stir, you can afford to introduce a bit of colour-blocking. Say your shirt's yellow – a beige skirt will provide some contrast without stealing any thunder. If your shirt is mint, a pair of chocolate brown trousers would be a brilliant plus one.

If in doubt, rely on jeans. I once fell head over heels in love with a blouse from Christopher John Rogers. It was the kitchen sink of blouses, made from flower-printed georgette, with asymmetric buttons and flamenco-style sleeves that would have made it near impossible to wash your hands, ironically. It was a statement and a half by anyone's definition and was styled with none other than baggy jeans. Perfection.

minimalism

STATEMENT DRESSING

Bowie was the master of making a statement. So many of his most memorable outfits contained some kind of exclamation point. By embracing this style of exuberance, you'll always have something to say with what you're wearing.

OFF-KILTER

Yamamoto's asymmetric bodysuits have got to be some of the most iconic stage outfits of all time. They were so extraordinary to look at, of course, because of the entirely naked opposing limbs. While you'd be hard pressed to find a similar silhouette off the rack – and even harder pressed to find an occasion which might warrant such a look – there's no shortage of tops that are more interesting for being in some way misaligned. In my opinion, the easiest styles to pull off are a bodysuit with a skew-whiff neckline, or a button-down shirt with a wonky hem.

MICROMANAGE

Bowie's legs got a lot of air time in the seventies. So if you haven't shown your thighs since your school days, there's no time like the present to take the plunge. A miniskirt is its own kind of statement, but it needs a firm hand if you want to give it a grown-up sensibility. Firstly, I would always wear it with sheer black tights. Secondly, you want to style it with something of a non-event to provide all-important balance. Prada has some of the best minis in the business – which soar well towards the upper thigh – and the guests outside the show tend to wear them with something unexpectedly sensible, like a navy jumper.

BIG-PERSONALITY SLEEVES

A sculpted shoulder and a full sleeve were all signatures of Ziggy's, but it's a trend his creator never lost sight of throughout his career. Performing in 1997, Bowie appeared wearing a loose white shirt with unbuttoned cuffs, which flared over his hands as he lunged with the microphone. You can channel a similar energy for everyday by choosing a white shirt with a side order of personality. What used to be a wardrobe staple has undergone something of a vibe shift over the past few years, and you can now buy versions with the addition of cutaway shoulders, a ruffled yoke or a puritanically high neck.

GREAT HEIGHTS

A remarkably whittled waist was another refrain in Bowie's wardrobe – and it was usually created with trousers, of all things. On the back cover of *Hunky Dory*, he wore a pair of beige trousers that could have been ordinary but were anything but thanks to dramatically flared hems combined with a waistband that hugged the wearer. A pair of high-rise jeans is a great entry point to this particular silhouette. I do it with the most amazing straight-legged style from E.L.V. Denim, a sustainable brand that uses 100 per cent upcycled denim, which fastens a few inches above my belly button. When I first looked in the mirror, I thought they looked strangely indecent because so much of my body was leg and very little wasn't, but once you get used to the balance it's hard to go back.

XL COLLARS

Bowie as Pierrot, a
metamorphosis which
involved a spangled blue suit
created by Natasha Korniloff, was
more costume than outfit. But you
could still cherry pick elements – like the
collar – and make them everyday. You don't
have to choose a collar of clown-like
proportions to make a statement; instead, seek
out styles with elegantly long points.

SHOW-OFF OUTERWEAR

Bowie's later stage outfits incorporated a lot of statement outerwear. Performing in 2002, he wore a single-breasted coat that was a particularly searing scarlet. It flared a few inches below his knee, which instantly reminded me of a look he wore in 1974. Photographed before a press conference at the Amstel Hotel, Amsterdam, Bowie looked magnificent in a dressing gown coat made of a stiff fabric that meant it held its shape to his mid-calf. Because of its silhouette and the camera's angle, he looked incredibly tall, almost like he was standing on stilts. The moral of the story is that if you choose a coat that's enough of a statement, you will look sensational without having to worry about what you're wearing underneath.

FIND YOUR
OWN

AND

YNY

ROG

'He could look alien-like or female-like; it was always so exciting as everything he did was so unpredictable.'

TERRY O'NEILL

W hen Harry Styles shimmies onto a stage wearing a feather boa with a butterfly-tattooed bare chest, nobody bats an eyelid. In fact, the accessory once associated with hen-do humiliation has become so deeply ingrained in the psyche of his following that there was nothing short of a 'feather boa massacre' on the pavements after the first of his two performances in Cardiff in 2023, according to the BBC. Of course, Bowie did it 50 years earlier.

Bowie's feather boa was a frequent companion of his during 1973. Bright turquoise, and as bold as the colour of his hair, it was often wrapped around his slender neck when he was wearing the one-sleeved knitted jumpsuit by Kansai Yamamoto. It was another piece of the puzzle – like the patent platform boots, the single crystal earring and the giant bangles around his wrists and ankles – that contributed to his alien creation's androgynous mystique.

From the countless anecdotes in Jones' *David Bowie: A Life*, it's clear that Angie, Bowie's first wife – who he was married to for that crucial decade between 1970 and 1980 – was a driving force behind his fluid approach to style, that, to the naked eye, looked neither strictly male nor strictly female. Paul Reeves, the fashion designer and owner of Fulham Road's Universal Witness, went as far as to say that Bowie 'would not have made it without Angie'. Reeves continued: 'When he suddenly announced he was gay, that was Angie. That was her doing. She styled him, she put him in women's clothes, she was the one who understood androgyny.' At the time, she was a bit of everything to Bowie – a wife, a facilitator, a stylist, a co-creator – and it was her uncanny ability to take the temperature of what was not exactly fashion, but what was exciting, that helped turn her then-husband into an alien superstar, Ziggy Stardust.

Of course, Bowie knew what he was doing. He used to claim that what he wore was a man's dress not a woman's dress. But it was still a dress. And it was still thrillingly outré, even if you were part of the glam-rocker subset and no stranger to wearing a smudge of eyeliner. After all, Mick Jagger wore a dress two years ahead of Bowie. Everyone was doing it. Bowie just did it a bit better.

After cycling through the identities of Ziggy Stardust, Aladdin Sane and Halloween Jack, Bowie's stage wardrobe shifted into an almost naturalistic gear in comparison, but he kept up his experimentations with androgyny. Glam rock might have been in his rearview mirror as he headed to Los Angeles, but that was by no means the end of the make-up, the hair dye, the nail polish or – you guessed it – the dresses.

There were the rather spectacular drag looks in the video for *Boys Keep Swinging*, which was released in 1979. That same year, Bowie brought his brand of alt-magic to *Saturday Night Live*. As well as sharing the stage with a candy pink poodle and two legendary performance artists, Klaus Nomi and Joey Arias, Bowie's set included puppet wizardry and a rather stern grey skirt suit designed by Brooks Van Horn, which he wore with a boyish combover to sing *TVC15*. A 'Chinese Communist air-hostess look' was how he characterised it to *Rolling Stone*. It was something entirely different to the otherworldly androgyny of Ziggy, but was no less compelling.

HIS ANDROGYNOUS PIECES

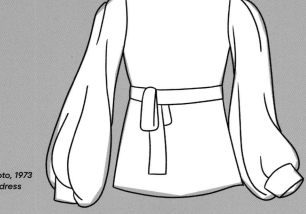

Kansai Yamamoto, 1973
- white kimono dress

It wasn't all about dresses, although they often get star-billing because of the sheer shock-factor. Bowie also managed to bring an element of androgyny to the everyday. A T-shirt became a blank canvas for rebellion, something sexy and subversive. You can parlay a similar energy into your existing wardrobe simply by tweaking the rules ever-so-slightly when it comes to what goes with what.

DRESSES

In 1972, Bowie was interviewed by the editor of *Melody Maker*, Michael Watts. At some point, the journalist asked, 'Why aren't you wearing your girl's dress today?' Bowie replied: 'Oh dear. You must understand that it's not a woman's. It's a man's dress.' Bowie was perhaps falling into the role of provocateur, but he did wear dresses as Ziggy. (There was the little white kimono by Kansai Yamamoto, which was revealed onstage as part of a quick costume change. It was so short that he frequently flashed the bulge of his crotch, which brings us back to the 'man's dress' comment, although the designer helpfully included what appeared to be a built-in pair of satin briefs to protect the star's modesty.) But there was also the dress by Michael Fish, which he's wearing to lounge on a chaise for the cover of *The Man Who Sold The World*, with its gorgeously flaring skirt and keyhole cut-outs.

Takeaways: If you're wearing a dress that's dainty or simply in danger of looking twee, you need a certain kind of plus one. Bowie's kimono was worn with thigh-high satin boots. A modern reinterpretation might be knee-high biker boots, or Dr. Martens, which will add a certain heft to a lofty hemline. A sturdy brogue, worn with a wool ankle sock, is another way to do it. Birkenstock's Boston clog is also excellent at taking a ruffled neckline or a flounced hem in an interesting direction, but you can also play around with a more androgynous layer. A puffy-sleeved white prairie dress would instantly look more effortless with pinstripe trousers underneath, or an oversized blazer thrown around the shoulders.

BODYSUITS

Bowie's lithe thighs were often exposed to the elements as Ziggy, which was usually because he was wearing a bodysuit, a leotard or a skin-tight creation of some kind. The Kansai Yamamoto playsuit was particularly striking, with its short sleeves, scoop-neck and searing-red colour. In what was a fantastically surreal moment of television, Bowie sent a kind of surrogate to 2014's BRIT Awards: Kate Moss, who was wearing none other than the barely-there red onesie to accept the gong on his behalf for Best British Male. The model styled it differently, adding a pair

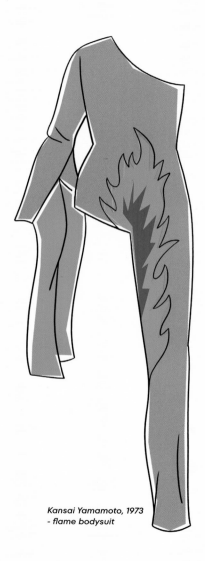

*Kansai Yamamoto, 1973
- flame bodysuit*

of shoulder-grazing earrings, black tights and startlingly tall platform boots from Vivienne Westwood. But it looked just as good on Moss as it did on the barefoot Bowie.

The silver leotard is another example of androgyny in action. It had a swooping neckline that cleaved to Bowie's chest, and silvery fringed sleeves that looked like tinsel. It's actually one of the few times he wore sequins, which weren't a signature part of his repertoire, and the effect conjured by the fringe moving back and forth must have been mesmerising.

Takeaways: A bodysuit is a tremendously useful item of clothing, so much so that it doesn't usually get much of a showing because it's positioned underneath something like a trouser suit. Lingerie brands make the best bodysuits, because of their attention to detail when it comes to technical fabrics and a glove-like fit. Try Falke, Marks & Spencer, Wolford and SKIMS, the latter of which is faultless in its range of sizes and silhouettes – from the simple to the more statement-making. To emphasise the fact that you're wearing a bodysuit, you could either style it with a semi-sheer skirt so that you can see its outline underneath, or with low-slung trousers so that a triangle of bare skin emerges on each hip.

T-SHIRT AND TROUSERS

What could be more foundational than a pair of trousers and a T-shirt? In the hands of David Bowie on the Low/Heroes Tour, the combination became a *coup de théâtre*. The entire look was masterminded by Natasha Korniloff, who obviously had an appreciation for the fact that an androgynous element here or there could add something of interest to the most basic of garments.

First of all, the waistband was high. I mean, *extremely* high. This was something of a signature for Bowie. For his famously flirtatious performance with Cher, grooving and grinning side-by-side as they sang *Young Americans*, he wore a simple pair of slacks that had an impressively high waistband, making his legs look even longer. He went even further for the Low/Heroes Tour, with trousers that not only hugged his tiny waist but swelled out at the hips to create a silhouette that you don't often see with a men's trouser. The T-shirt, of course, contributed to the effect because of its fabulously fitted shape.

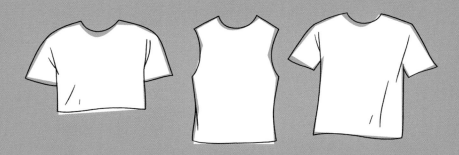

Takeaways: You, too, can play on the androgyny of the most basic items of clothing by exaggerating one part of the body. A T-shirt and a pair of high-waisted trousers is one way, but you could also swap the top half for a muscle tee – a boxy, sleeveless tank top with slanted shoulders that can be worn tighter or looser depending on the effect you want to create. Wear an oversized version with a miniskirt, say, and it will immediately make the ensemble look more effortless. You can also create a similar contrast with a starched white shirt that's a couple of sizes too big.

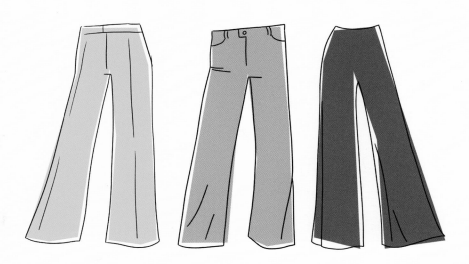

ALWAYS
ADD

MORE MORE MORE
MORE MORE MORE
MORE MORE MORE
MORE MORE MORE
MORE MORE MORE
MORE MORE MORE
MORE MORE MORE
MORE MORE MORE
MORE MORE MORE
MORE MORE MORE
MORE MORE MORE

'Bowie was like a cat: he was strutting about, he was being provocative, he was grinning … He was everything and everywhere.'

EDDIE CLARKE

Most Bowie creations had a defining accessory. Perhaps these accessories helped him get into character before heading onstage, like the set of braces he wore for the Serious Moonlight Tour. You can almost imagine him loosening his collar, making sure the knot of his striped tie was positioned just so, before stepping on stage. And what about the sailor's cap that he wore while touring in 1978? You also can't ignore the solitary crystal earring, or the set of tubular bangles he adopted as Ziggy. These proved beyond a doubt that an accessory could provide a sense of balance as well as a sense of theatre. The tubular bangles were worn with the famous asymmetric bodysuit designed by Kansai Yamamoto, which revealed the entirety of the singer's right leg and left arm. His limbs would have looked strangely naked were it not for the flashes of red, green and gold that the bangles offered.

If that makes it sound like a calculated process, it wasn't. Bowie tended to gravitate towards certain accessories, wear them to death, then discard them and move on. It was an instinctual part of trying on different identities for him (and was usually done with a sense of humour).

In the kaleidoscopic documentary *Moonage Daydream*, which was made with permission from Bowie's estate, television interviews are spliced together with footage from concerts to mesmeric effect. One of the clips is from a sit-down interview with Russell Harty. Bowie is holding court as Ziggy, while the man opposite him stares bemusedly. After Bowie rather earnestly describes the shift in societal mores between his father's generation and his own, when people were beginning to strive for the individual, Harty points at his feet and asks: 'Are those men's shoes or women's shoes or bisexual shoes?' Bowie doesn't miss a beat. 'They're shoe shoes, silly.'

BOWIEŚ SHOES

Elvis had his blue suede shoes. Bowie, on the other hand, had a penchant for all manner of footwear, flat and heeled, practical and playful. (His most commercially successful song, after all, is about red shoes.)

In Jones' *David Bowie: A Life*, Legs McNeil, a music journalist, recalled a telling piece of advice from Mick Jagger. 'Never wear a new pair of shoes in front of him.' McNeil interpreted this sentence quite simply: Bowie would most likely buy them, and by doing so, claim credit for being a pioneer of the trend, whether inadvertently or intentionally. (As detailed in Tom Hagler's book, *Bowie at the BBC: A Life in Interviews*, Bowie later clarified the matter in an interview with *BBC Radio*, explaining that Jagger made this comment because Bowie had nicked Guy Peellaert, the artist who worked on one of his most famous album covers, from Jagger: 'He never forgave me for that, because mine was *Diamond Dogs* and I can't remember what his was.')

He had an early predilection for good shoes, particularly if they were Italian. In the same interview with *BBC Radio*, he told an anecdote about his childhood pride at being the first fourteen-year-old in the area, along with his friend George, to own high pointers by Denson's. 'Yeah, I'm big on shoes,' he said. 'And then we were pipped by a much smoother guy in the sixth form called Gavin. [...] He had Chelsea boots. They were so kind of elegant because they weren't pointed and they had elastic sides. We were so crestfallen.'

Despite being outdone by smooth Gavin, Bowie persevered, collecting a shoedrobe over his career that included heeled brogues, patent platform boots, satin thigh-highs and winged cowboy boots. Bowie mastered the art of what you could call a 'final outfit flourish' – a well-chosen cherry on top that would take a look from ordinary to extraordinary – and it often started with his feet. Perhaps it was because he knew that the fans gathered closest to the stage would be roughly at eye level with his shoes, but his taste constantly evolved with his characters, creating a truly spectacular back catalogue. He even wore a pair of stiletto-heeled boots to meet Tony Blair. As Bowie joked to Jeremy Paxman on *Newsnight* – who brought up the subject of politicians hugging rock stars – it was his way of sticking two fingers to the man. 'I do my bit, still. He didn't even notice, you know.'

PATENT PLATFORM BOOTS

Bowie wasn't actually that tall, standing at 1.77m, but thanks to the combination of his yoga-toned limbs and platform boots, he looked statuesque as Ziggy. He had the famous patent pair made by Anello and Davide, based on a design of Kansai Yamamoto's, and they were so tight, they looked like they were suctioned to his legs, and they were so red, they radiated kink. They were made for a museum retrospective. This doesn't mean that you couldn't try something similar, though. I would suggest forgoing red for black, and knee-high for ankle length. A pointed toe paired with a kitten heel will lend a similar sense of fun, while being somewhat easier to walk (or strut) in.

SILVER BALLET PUMPS

For the cover of *Ashes to Ashes*, Bowie cast himself as the sad clown. As well as wearing an ice blue suit with puffed sleeves and pantaloons, he held one of his silver ballet pumps to his ear as if it was a telephone. The accompanying music video is a phantasmagorical masterpiece, as weird as it is wonderful, making his rather traditional shoe choice even more interesting. Ballet flats have had something of a revival since their heyday in the early two-thousands, largely thanks to new-gen designer versions from The Row, Miu Miu and Alaïa. I would argue that the high street gives as good as it gets when it comes to this particular shoe, offering classic styles that won't date, as well as versions with a similar metallic chutzpah to Bowie's.

High street brands for good quality ballet pumps:

★ Arket

★ Boden

★ John Lewis

★ Massimo Dutti

★ River Island

★ Zara

COWBOY BOOTS

On his Glass Spider Tour, Bowie was almost in rockabilly mode, wearing lots of leather, metallics, and a pair of winged cowboy boots, all curated by Diana Moseley. You'd be hard-pressed to find a front row these days that doesn't feature this style of boot – Western with stitching, a slanted heel and plenty of swagger. But as well as the extra variety, the high street has plenty of everyday styles that you can wear with jeans, black trousers or a midi dress, so they disappear beneath the hem. You can find good quality leather and suede versions at & Other Stories, COS, Hush and Whistles, as well as on resale platforms like Vinted.

WHY SHOES MATTER

When I'm getting dressed, I often start with shoes, because they're the gateway to understanding what you want your look to say. Bowie's shoes were carefully considered. He often went for a 'more is more' approach as Ziggy – wearing a snappy suit with a sculptural platform sandal and lurex sock – but he also knew how to dial it back down with an Oxford shoe.

Your shoe choice can also totally change the direction of an outfit, pulling it back from looking too preppy, for example. That's why so-called 'ugly' shoes – like clogs or hiking sandals worn with socks – can be such a gift if you want to look a little offbeat. My chosen pair are from Penelope Chilvers – and they're not ugly at all. Far from it in fact. They're black leather clogs with a silver horsebit, and they make any outfit – from wide-leg jeans with a bouclé jacket and baseball cap, to a puff-sleeved dress – look so much more interesting.

HOW TO PICK AN APPROPRIATE ADD-ON

Bowie's stage ensembles and their accoutrements weren't meant to be worn in real life. They were costumes, first and foremost. But that doesn't mean you can't borrow a bit of their theatricality to bring a point of interest to an everyday outfit.

JEWELLERY

EARRINGS

Bowie probably doesn't strike you as a man of
moderation in most respects, but he toed the line very
carefully between excess and exactly the right amount.
It's this sense of balance that gives an outfit intrigue.
As Halloween Jack, Bowie looked halfway between a rock
star and a pirate in party mode, wearing an eye patch
(initially not a fashion statement but a solution to hiding
the fact he had conjunctivitis), a single hoop earring and
a printed silk scarf. Once again, he was ahead of his time.
As Ziggy, as well as at the 1996 BRIT Awards, one ear was
pierced with a cascade of crystals that almost grazed
his shoulder. Wearing mismatched earrings has become
mainstream in recent years, as more and more people
opt for a twinkling constellation instead of coordinating
sets. I would shop from brands who make purposely
asymmetric pairs like Completedworks, whose modern
pearl and cubic zirconia creations are always striking,
as well as high street shops like COS, H&M and Zara.

BROOCHES

In *Labyrinth*, Bowie looked like an iridescent nobleman
with his silvery eye sockets, sequinned doublet, frilled
blouse and glittery brooch as Jareth, the Goblin King.

You don't see many people wearing pins these days, but they're ideal for adding another layer of interest to an outfit. Picture a plain black trouser suit. So far, so boring. But introduce a brooch on its left lapel, something sculptural or sparkly, and you've instantly created a conversation-starter.

ACCESSORIES

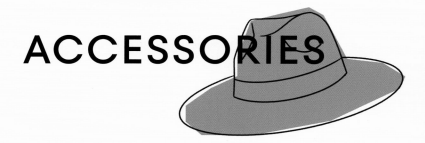

HATS

I don't think anyone looks as good in hats as David Bowie, who wore sailor's caps, flat caps and fedoras with aplomb. At the Grammy Awards in 1975, his slanted hat cast a shadow over the unusually dilated pupil of his left eye, making him look even more mesmerising. And then, of course, there's *The Man Who Fell to Earth*, which incidentally came out five years before *Raiders of the Lost Ark*. (In my opinion, the fedora's potential to make its wearer smoulder owes much more to Thomas Jerome Newton, the alien charged with a mission on planet Earth, than Indiana Jones.) Bowie wore a taupe version with a black band, letting it slope so that it showed one sculpted eyebrow and both sets of cheekbones (he eventually gifted it to Moby, who sadly lost it after inviting a few friends over to his house for drinks). Ola Hudson's costume design was so exceptional, in fact, that you could wear his entire wardrobe – the high-collared shirts, the wool coats, the nipped-waist and flared-leg suits and, yes, the fedoras – today.

SCARVES

Interestingly, Bowie waited to embrace what you might think of as a traditional rock 'n' roll aesthetic until the latter half of his career. At 2004's Isle of Wight Festival he sang a rousing rendition of *Rebel Rebel*. His outfit of choice was a ragged corduroy tailcoat with several scarfs knotted around his neck. It can't have been a coincidence that one year earlier, Alexander McQueen introduced a printed skull scarf as part of its spring/summer 2003 collection, which was quickly adopted by the decade's influencers (Mary-Kate Olsen used to wear three looped once around her neck so that they trailed down her front).

It's a tricky look to pull off without looking like you're wearing a costume. But a square silk scarf – the kind that you'll find by the basket-load in charity shops or vintage boutiques – can look chic yet cool with a simple outfit of a white tee and a vintage leather jacket. Kate Moss did it best in 2005, looping a long strip of red material around her neck that somehow pulled her military jacket, vest top and low-slung jeans together.

'The only statement that I can make visually with clothes that is not fashion is this.'

DAVID BOWIE

The *Heroes* album cover is undoubtedly less provocative than, say, *Diamond Dogs* (where the rock star's slender body morphs into a canine's from the neck down). It's also less overtly virulent than *Let's Dance*, where Bowie is buff, topless and boxing.

Nevertheless, *Heroes* is one of Bowie's most beloved album covers, and it's striking because of his intensely alert eyes and hands, which were a homage to German Expressionist Erich Heckel. In the outtakes from the shoot, in which he was photographed by long-time collaborator Masayoshi Sukita, Bowie is variously smoking, tousling his hair, grimacing, covering his face and smiling rather ruefully. In every one, he's wearing the same leather jacket from Aero Leather – a snugly fitting blouson with its collar flipped towards the throat. It was minimal and sexy. As a fan, you couldn't have held that record without feeling a frisson or a voice from within telling you, 'I need that jacket.'

Ironically, Bowie himself didn't consider that staple of the rock 'n' roller wardrobe as fashion. In fact, he felt the opposite. In 1987, almost a decade after *Heroes*, he was interviewed by *Vox Pop*. The journalist complimented his 'look' – a leather jacket. Bowie replied, 'This is totally non-fashion – it's timeless, and I feel very comfortable in it, doing what I'm doing, writing the music that I'm writing. And of course I've always worn this jacket.'

JACKETS

It makes sense that Bowie saw the leather jacket as a second skin. It was a kind of uniform, after all, or perhaps even armour. His heroes wore them (Little Richard, Elvis and John Lennon), and so did his contemporaries (Mick Jagger, Iggy Pop and Freddie Mercury). It should probably be included on the itemised list of 'sex, drugs and rock 'n' roll.' It's certainly as synonymous with the hard-living lifestyle as the first two.

Bowie might have called it 'non-fashion', classing it as a bread-and-butter wardrobe perennial, but a leather jacket is subject to trends as well as being timeless. In the nineties and early two-thousands, biker styles with zippers and hardware started to dominate. The oversized blouson with minimal bells and whistles, as well as aviator-style bombers, have both experienced a resurgence. Naturally, the best place to find 'the one' is in vintage shops or on resale sites.

Bowie wore his leather jacket with shirts and slacks, which is as timeless as the jacket itself, but you can also play around and pair it with something slightly more unexpected, like a tulle skirt or a pair of track pants.

OUTFIT IDEAS

A leather jacket is a brilliant building block that's very useful to have in your outerwear rotation. It's naturally cool, yet an exceptionally hard-worker, adding an effortless kind of energy to anything you can throw at it. It can even claim a place in the workwear side of your wardrobe, making a box-pleated skirt, or simple wool trousers look less corporate because of their proximity to something ever-so-slightly rock 'n' roll.

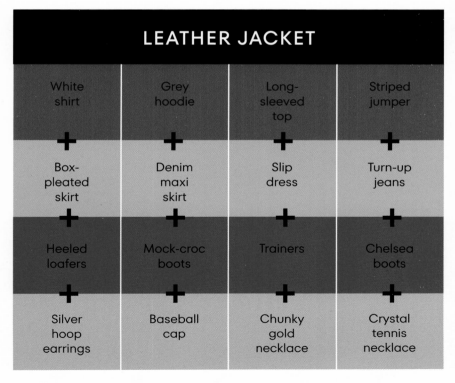

LEATHER JACKET

White shirt	Grey hoodie	Long-sleeved top	Striped jumper
+	+	+	+
Box-pleated skirt	Denim maxi skirt	Slip dress	Turn-up jeans
+	+	+	+
Heeled loafers	Mock-croc boots	Trainers	Chelsea boots
+	+	+	+
Silver hoop earrings	Baseball cap	Chunky gold necklace	Crystal tennis necklace

THE LEATHER LOOK

Of course, jackets are just the tip of the iceberg when it comes to wearing leather. Despite the hefty price tag, even high street brands are making leather shirts, skirts, trousers, dresses, and even trench coats, which might cost four figures but will stand the test of time in your wardrobe. There are also plenty of faux-leather options, although it's always best to buy in person so that you can examine the fabric's quality.

SKIRTS

Denim has the edge over leather on most occasions. As well as being more comfortable to wear, it somehow looks less intentional and more effortless. But choose the right length and there's something to be said for a leather skirt. It dials up the drama, even if worn with something everyday, like a crisp white shirt, a grey cashmere sweater or a simple long-sleeved top. Less is more is always the modus operandi at 16Arlington – one of the hottest designer brands to come out of London – who cuts its straight leather skirts off at the knee. It's a tricky length to master, because you almost certainly need to pair it with a heel to avoid shortening the length of your legs. If you prefer flats, I'd opt instead for a swishing maxi skirt.

Nanushka makes the best in the business, and they're not actually leather at all, but are made of a 100 per cent recycled polyester product called Okobor™ Alt-leather. There are also just-as-good options on the high street. I rate Massimo Dutti, Arket and COS, whose leather skirts always feel buttery soft. For faux leather, it's got to be Zara, who has a knack for making it look like the real deal. Because the fabric naturally has a tendency to look 'done', I would always suggest paring it back with something lo-fi like a rugby shirt or a sweater vest.

TROUSERS

Leather trousers have gone through almost as many metamorphoses as Bowie, evolving from straight in the nineties to skinny in the two-thousands. They've now gone full circle, of course, returning to a looser, cooler and more comfortable silhouette that mirrors the trajectory of jeans. Bottega Veneta's leather trousers are big, slouchy and styled with knitwear that's similarly XL. Bowie, however, would perhaps prefer the interpretations at Alexander McQueen, whose version is whip-smart and polished, sitting high on the waist. When he wore leather trousers for the Low/Heroes World Tour, the overall look was almost the antithesis of Ziggy Stardust – scrubbed of obvious make-up, swathed in a baggy white shirt and high-waisted leather combat trousers. Of course this was another revelation – a pairing that somehow looks contemporary even though it was 1978. Just remember to strike the same balance with your top and bottom halves when you try it.

COATS

A leather coat is an investment purchase, but one that will genuinely only get better with time as the material ages into that lived-in look. I'm a big believer in the fact that there's a leather coat for every aesthetic. If you subscribe to a no-muss, no-fuss minimalism, look for a single-breasted leather coat that is straight up and down. For something form-fitting, try a double-breasted trench coat that you can belt at the waist or leave to flap open over tailoring. As for off-duty, seek out styles with shearling or faux-fur collar and cuffs.

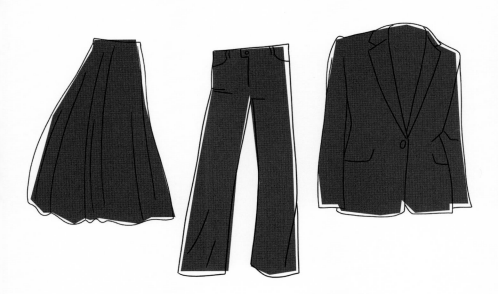

MAKE A
STATEMENT
IN

MON
OCHR
OME

'I have no time for glamour. It seems a ridiculous thing to strive for. I couldn't care less.'

DAVID BOWIE

Bowie is often thought of as Technicolour and it's true that he gravitated toward saturated shades. In 1991, on tour with his band Tin Machine, his costumes were almost entirely block colours: lemon, lime and a very specific shade of pink: Pepto Bismo. But black and white was a constant refrain in his wardrobe, a combination he started wearing in earnest as the Thin White Duke. This was one of his more controversial characters, a much darker persona than, say, the glam-rock messenger Ziggy Stardust, and the Thin White Duke's clothes were fittingly noir: a stark white shirt and black tuxedo trousers designed by Ol Hudson, who Bowie also worked with on *The Man Who Fell To Earth*. The *Station to Station* album cover was his first in monochrome, his suited figure peering through a wall of foam stalagmites, and the only colour a line of blood red writing that ran across the top.

The Thin White Duke soon hung up his proverbial hat, but black and white was never relegated to the archives. Three years later, Bowie brought out *Lodger*, where he's photographed on a white tiled floor, his limbs askew, his hand bandaged and his nose broken. A human splat wearing a black suit. Never had the colour combination looked so intriguing.

The Blind Prophet was Bowie's last character, appearing with bandages wrapped around his head and buttons for eyes in the video for *Lazarus*, as well as *Blackstar*, in which he wore a black frock coat over a white shirt with loose cuffs. It was the opposite to the Thin White Duke, who was sharp and starched. The final album cover was literally a black star on a white background, perhaps a sign that Bowie, who had spent so much of his career as the showman, intended to go out with a different kind of bang.

THE ULTIMATE COLOUR COMBINATION

Certain colour combinations are considered particularly 'fashion', like red and pink, but the ultimate, the one that gets revisited season after season, has got to be black and white. Far from fading into the background, it's a pairing that creates a sense of being cool and collected. The people who don't seek attention, but nonetheless make you look twice often wear black and white. (Rei Kawakubo, the enigmatic founder of Comme des Garçons, is one such person.) Black and white is also a trick deployed by celebrity stylists. If your talent is leaving a hotel or standing on the step-and-repeat in front of a busy backing board, bright colours can compete for attention with their surroundings, creating a messy final shot. Black and white, on the other hand, is clean and crisp, simple and stand-out.

So many designers, from the old establishment to the new guard, use the combination to great effect on the catwalk, including Alaïa, Chloé, Dior, Ferragamo, Issey Miyake and Jil Sander. Anthony Vaccarello's Saint Laurent has practically become a paean to the pairing, with celebrities flocking to his shows wearing black, white or both. In fact, his spring/summer 2024 menswear collection looked very much like a homage not just to the colour combination, but to the Thin White Duke, with one model sporting orange hair that was slicked to his scalp.

Tailoring is one of the most bankable ways to wear black and white. You just need to include some clever details – a flared hem here, an exaggerated shoulder there – so that it doesn't look like too much of an anodyne take on workwear.

You can also base lots of outfits around a white T-shirt. My favourite is from the menswear section of Uniqlo, which has elongated sleeves as well as an oversized fit. I wear mine with everything from black combat trousers to beige skirts with stiff pleats.

BLACK AND WHITE TAILORING FOR DIFFERENT BODY SHAPES

T RIA NGLE

Triangle body shapes tend to have wider hips than shoulders, creating a slightly more bottom-heavy silhouette. Choosing a **cropped jacket** and a pair of **high-waisted trousers** will accentuate your waist while lengthening your legs. I'd also opt for a **white tank top** instead of a shirt and would be tempted to add a **platform boot**, not unlike the curved-sole pair in *The Man Who Fell To Earth*, to give you a modest boost in the height department. You want your hems to just skim the floor.

UPSIDE-DOWN TRIANGLE

As an upside-down triangle with broader shoulders than hips, it might sound counterintuitive to accentuate your top half. But, trust me, it'll look intentional if you opt for an **off-white blazer** with either padded or ever-so-slightly sculpted shoulders. Pair it with a **leather pencil skirt** that stops a few inches below the knee, **sheer black tights** and **point-toe pumps** for a look that's sexy and sharp, all at once.

133

HOURGLASS

An hourglass figure nips in at the waist so that's the area you want to draw the eye towards. You can do this a couple of ways, but a piece that's become increasingly popular over the past few years is a **waistcoat**. It's a good entry point to tailoring – not as immersive, say, as a full-blown trouser or skirt suit – and can be styled with a pair of **double-pleated wool trousers** that stretch beyond the ankle bone and **smart leather loafers**.

OAVL

Those with an oval shape should look for **single-breasted blazers** – less boxy than double – that are cut to brush the upper thigh. A gently **flaring pair of suit trousers**, meanwhile, will create an hourglass effect, especially if worn with **kitten-heeled slingbacks**.

WEARING TOP-TO-TOE COLOUR

On 1987's Glass Spider Tour, Bowie wore costumes designed by Diana Moseley, one of which was a tomato-red trouser suit styled with silver-capped boots that were of a similarly acidic shade. Play-sparring on stage during a rendition of *Fashion*, the outfit certainly made an impact, especially with his feathery blond mullet, more ash than peroxide, that was coiffed by Teddy Antolin.

It wasn't the first time he'd worn one colour top-to-toe. For 1978's Low/Heroes Tour, Bowie wore the alluring combination of a simple tee and sailor trousers, both in white. It was the perfect stage outfit, striking against the set's pared-back design, and one that has the potential to work just as well in real life all these years later.

The trend for wearing monochrome – whether your shade of choice is butter or biscuit, canary or coffee – has become a standard flex in style circles. So much so that on the front rows at fashion month, celebrities will wear outfits that are almost entirely colour-coordinated, right down to their spaghetti-strapped sandals, their sunglasses and even their semi-sheer hosiery. And you don't even have to choose a 'main character' colour like tomato or turquoise. White, beige, grey or navy will work just as well. Seriously, try it. Not only will getting dressed every morning be much less of a headache, but colour-matching your clothes somehow makes every piece look miraculously polished.

GET A
SUIT
THAT

SUITS YOU

'With a suit, always wear big British shoes, the ones with large welts. There's nothing worse than dainty little Italian jobs at the end of the leg line.'

DAVID BOWIE

A trouser suit possesses a curious ability to transform from something boring to something quite breath-taking, depending on its colour, shape, shoulder width, leg length, lapel size or, often, a combination of all the above.

Bowie pretty much had a suit for each of his stage personalities, amassing a vast collection over his career. As an 18-year-old Mod, Bowie looked rather like every other teenager in 1965. Or, perhaps every other *fashion-conscious* teenager, wearing a black suit, a high-collared shirt, a skinny tie that he tucked into the waistband of his trousers and a full-fringed hairstyle that he copied from Keith Relf. As Bowie told *Rolling Stone*, he saved up to get one suit made at a tailors in Shepherd's Bush, the very same one as future glam-rocker Marc Bolan. He wouldn't wear his natural hair colour for a long time, but the suit was permitted to stay.

In the seventies, Bowie met Freddie Burretti.
It was totally by chance – Burretti simply
happened to be dancing in the same club as
Bowie – but he would go on to create some of
Bowie's most famous costumes of all time,
including the tri-coloured quilted two-piece
he wore to perform on that ground-breaking
1972 episode on *Top of the Pops*. The Bowie suit
canon would be decidedly less snappy without
the ice blue number in *Life on Mars?* And what
about the yellow suit he wore as the Soul Man?
Its English mustard meets ripe banana shade
gave it a retro flavour in hindsight, but it's still
zippy, particularly as he wore it with a stripy
shirt and socks.

He couldn't have gone in a more different
direction for 1975's Grammys. If you've read
about Bowie's outfit on paper, which was
designed by Jan Girard, you would have
assumed it was a traditional tuxedo, which it
was in a way. But Bowie managed to make

it look almost spectral, his cheeks shaded with bronzer to contrast with his pale skin, his red hair streaked with yellow and his fedora slanted jauntily over his larger left pupil. The jacket's exaggerated lapels also drew your eye to his waist, probably at its most whittled, while his trouser legs were noticeably flared. When he walked onto the stage to present the award for Best Rhythm and Blues Female Performance, he stopped several times on his way to the podium to bow like a conductor, getting an immediate peel of laughter when he opened his speech with, 'Ladies, gentlemen and others ...'. (He got another laugh when he put on a giant pair of sunglasses to read out the winner's name – Aretha Franklin.) Even when he was wearing a tuxedo, he managed to steal the show.

He did it again in 1983. Bowie had just arrived on a flight from Australia, where he was living at the time, to hold a press conference in London. It was a triumphant moment for the rock star, who had a room full of journalists eating out of the palm of his hand as he announced that he'd finished his new album and single, *Let's Dance*. He didn't sit on the chair provided in front of the microphones, but gamely hopped on the little table they were perched on. Despite presumably being discombobulated by jet-lag, he looked like an extraordinary version of an ordinary man, wearing a simple grey suit with an unbuttoned shirt collar. The look constituted something of a volte-face for Bowie. It was looser and more louche – the tantalising next step in his tailoring evolution.

Whether it was a lime green suit styled with a bare chest instead of a button-down, or a film-star tuxedo, Bowie always wore the suit – not the other way round.

A SUITS SPECTRUM

Bowie cycled through plenty of personalities, but many had a penchant for suits. In fact, Bowie's back catalogue has something for everyone, whether you're looking for tailoring that's classic, retro or even bridal.

CLASSIC

For 2002's performance at the Hammersmith Apollo (formerly the Hammersmith Odeon), Bowie turned to one of his favourite menswear designers. Hedi Slimane, who at the time was creative director of Dior Homme, promptly furnished him with a petrol-blue trouser suit that walked a fine line between regal and renegade, worn, as it was, with a watch chain, a black waistcoat and an undone collar. If you're looking for a suit that's elegant yet off-beat, you couldn't do better, especially as brighter blue shades are easing ahead of navy.

Vital stats: tailcoat-shaped blazer, slim-fit trousers, petrol blue.

LOUD

If you've never met a neutral that didn't make you yawn, what you need is an acid-bright blazer. In the early nineties, Bowie had a seriously zesty phase, sporting a neon green trouser suit by Thierry Mugler. It was a thrillingly astringent style move – and one that you could parlay into your own wardrobe simply by adding a squeeze of lime or lemon whenever it suits. (Bowie actually wore his blazer without a shirt when he was photographed by Brian Aris.) Not for the faint-hearted.

Vital stats: single-breasted, collarless, neon shade.

LOUCHE

Bowie's suiting bravado reached its zenith during his Serious Moonlight Tour, with a wardrobe of powder blue tailoring worn with braces and brash ties. The loose-legged trousers meant that when he sang *Let's Dance*, he wasn't messing around. This is a suit that will move with its wearer. Look for a fluid material, like a silk-blend georgette or a crepe de chine, making sure the waistband of your trousers sits as high as it can on your torso.

Vital stats: short jacket, high-waisted trousers, pastel shade.

BRIDAL

A white dress might be the opposite of your bridal personality. But what about a white suit? Arriving for a photoshoot in 1973, Bowie wore pearly white tailoring with satin lapels. He even accessorised with a crystal pin as a kind of corsage. It was a moment of reflection after the graphic mania of Ziggy, who he'd officially retired a few months earlier, and yet was still otherworldly. What could make more of a statement on your big day?

Vital stats: double-breasted blazer, exaggerated lapels, pearl white.

RETRO

The *Life on Mars?* suit is one of Bowie's most sublime, with a series of retro hallmarks that make it distinctly seventies. Designed by Freddie Burretti, its dazzling aqua shade rather blows black out of the water. It was the definition of snappy, especially with the metallic tie. Second-hand shops and vintage marketplaces will be the best places to look for suiting with arresting design details like contrast lapels, exaggerated shoulders or jazzy prints.

Vital stats: exaggerated lapels, turn-up trouser hems, retro shade.

HOW TO FIND A SUITABLE SILHOUETTE

With a triangular silhouette, a clever way to trick the eye is by choosing a blazer that's elongated so that it covers your bottom, bringing your shoulders and hips into alignment. You also want your trouser hems to brush or even pool on the floor, depending on your preference, so that your legs look as long as possible. If you need some height, opt for a gloved court pump, preferably in a contrasting shade. It's cooler than a traditional court and tends to have a more comfortable block heel.

UPSIDE-DOWN TRIANGLE

As an upside-down triangle, your shoulders will be slightly wider than your hips. A fun way to counter a top-heavy silhouette is by wearing a mismatched trouser suit. By positioning a darker colour on top and a contrasting colour on the bottom, the eye isn't being confronted with one solid block. Just how contrasting you go is entirely up to you, but some fun combinations could be camel and red, black and tangerine or white and emerald.

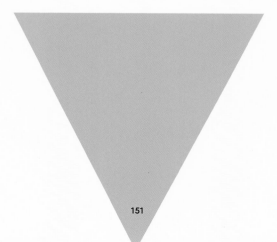

HOURGLASS

A Bermuda shorts suit is a very smart proposition for hourglass silhouettes, where your body has a defined waist. The best ones are slightly boyish in cut, while maintaining a high-waisted fit so that you're satisfyingly nipped in at your smallest point. You really want the shorts to stretch to your knees, while the blazer should ideally be single-breasted. You can play on the short suit's relaxed spirit by choosing a dressier shoe like Mary-Janes.

OVAL

A fun way to elongate your body is to experiment with a slight kick flare. A lot of trouser shapes gently crescendo because of the lengthening effect, although it doesn't have to be anything approaching Elvis-level. Just make sure your hems reach the ground instead of hovering around your ankles. If you don't want to wear a full trouser suit, you could also wear a jumper on top with a leather jacket. Shoes-wise, I'd be tempted by a pointed mule with a slender ankle strap or slingback. How high the heel should be is entirely up to you.

RECTANGLE

If your body doesn't go in-and-out at the waist, so your shoulders are roughly the same width as your hips, why not take a miniskirt suit for a spin? I would suggest buying the blazer a size up to make the whole effect slightly less 'done', while obviously making sure it doesn't eclipse your skirt. Once you've found your fit, it's a two-piece that does whatever you want it to do, depending on your choice of accessories. A T-bar flat is smart. A kitten-heeled slingback is sexy. Just add sheer tights if you want to wear her to the office.

WHAT TO WEAR

In the music video for *I'm Afraid of Americans*, Bowie is being pursued through the streets of New York. He's not exactly dressed for a high-speed chase, because he's wearing a paisley trouser suit with a chunky polo neck. His character might have regretted such an underlayer after several blocks of graceful sprinting, but his choice of knitwear was something of a revelation, particularly if you're looking for a step-change from shirting. It's not an appropriate plus one for slim-fit suiting, because your arms will be pinioned to your sides, but for an oversized wool suit like Bowie's, it can add a relaxed note that's decidedly anti-square. To suit the heft of a heavy-gauge knit, I would simply add a brogue-style boot.

On New York's social scene in the nineties, meanwhile, Bowie again wore his tailoring with turtlenecks, this time of a thinner wool variety. It was on these occasions that he also took the opportunity to wear one colour from top-to-toe, often a dove or charcoal grey that was cool and louche. You'll find that it's also a remarkably polished option for workwear. Try it when your everyday suit and shirt combo starts to feel a little lacklustre. (Note: Uniqlo's

UNDERNEATH

100 per cent Extra-Fine Merino Ribbed Turtleneck Jumper
– machine washable and available in more than 10
different shades – is the best option on the high street
for quality versus price point.)

Rewinding by roughly a decade to the Serious Moonlight
Tour, Bowie's wardrobe was a tour-de-force in tailoring,
orchestrated by costume maestro Peter J. Hall. It was a
little like looking at the world through rose-tinted glasses
– the colour palette was dreamily soft, while the shapes
were altogether looser: lightyears away from Ziggy.
Leaning into this new mood, Hall decided to pair the
suits with open-collared shirts, an undone bow tie draped
around the neck. The effect wasn't scruffy but kind of …
sexy. Neckties have been all but phased out of most
offices, bar boardroom meetings, but no one says you
can't wear one as a fashion statement (the business-
casual dress code be damned). You could opt for a skinny
black style like sixties Bowie, but for a truer imitation of his
eighties approach to tailoring, seek out a striped tie that
you can knot then strategically loosen to your liking.

Bowie kept the loose necktie, but added another element
to his tailoring looks in the two-thousands – a fitted
waistcoat, which of course was a signature of an earlier
character: the Thin White Duke. It became a modern kind
of rock star uniform when worn with a petrol-blue tailcoat.
I would suggest creating a new kind of three-piece with
your waistcoat, pairing it with a blazer but switching out
the suit trousers for indigo jeans.

Bowie carefully preserved all of his stage costumes, including his suits, so you've got no excuse to not be as painstaking.

NIPS AND TUCKS

A suit always looks best if it's perfectly tailored, which means you're likely to need a nip or a tuck at some point or another. For simple repairs or alterations, you can usually rely on your local dry-cleaner. The alternative is a nationwide app like Sojo, which offers a menu of tailoring, alteration and repair services within a week, and The Seam, which connects customers to local makers.

STEAMER

Most, if not all, suits will be dry-clean only. But if your jacket just needs a two-second refresh after being folded in a suit carrier, try using a hand-held steamer, which will quickly smooth out the creases. Steamery is the number-one choice of steamer for stylish travellers.

MOTHS

There's nothing worse than pulling out your wool suit only to find it's looking a little worse for wear (read: savaged by moths). After getting to the bottom of the problem, put cedar blocks in your cupboards and drawers – the wood's scent is a natural repellent and a good preventative measure.

SWITCH
UP
YOUR

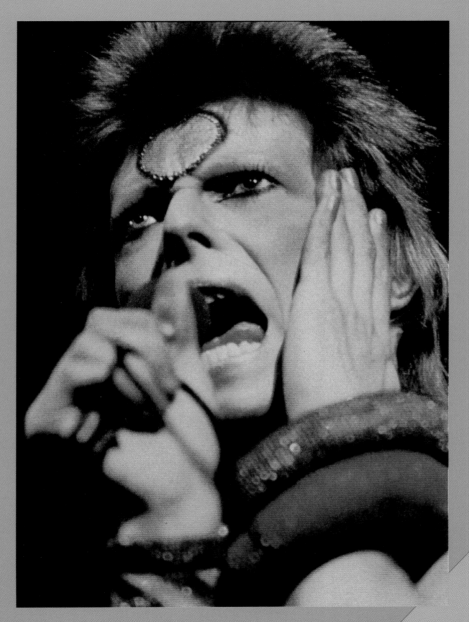

SWITCH UP YOUR MAKE-UP

David Bowie:
'Do you like all this
glam rock stuff?'

John Lennon:
'Yeah, it's great.
Well, it's just rock
'n' roll with lipstick
on, isn't it?'

Hair meant a great deal to David Bowie. As an adolescent, he and his associates were part of an organisation called 'The Society for the Prevention of Cruelty to Long-Haired Men,' which defended the rights of men who refused to submit to the barber's chair. It might have been a private joke between friends, but perhaps it was also a sign of what was to come, because I'd wager that not many rock stars could be identified by a pencil outline of their most famous haircut alone. Bowie was also a fearless experimenter. There were simply no limits to his willingness to be a blank canvas.

Then, of course, there's the make-up. It's no surprise that the album cover for *Aladdin Sane*, shot by Brian Duffy, is Bowie's most iconic cover of all time. What was a surprise to me was that the reason for its place in history – the lightning bolt zig-zagging across his face, soaring over his forehead, eye socket and cheekbone with its perfectly electrifying shades of red and blue

– wasn't exactly planned. It's true that it was partly based on Elvis Presley's TCB, the lightning-bolt logo that incorporated his catchphrase, 'Taking Care of Business', but it was also inspired, remarkably, by a rice cooker that happened to be in the studio's kitchen at the time of the shoot, which also had a lightning-bolt logo according to Chris Duffy, Brian Duffy's son, speaking to *AnOther Magazine*. It wasn't paint but lipstick – hence the high-shine slick – that contrasted beautifully with the pearlescent sheen of Bowie's skin, created by Pierre La Roche.

Even when he moved away from glam rock, having brought the era to its zenith and made himself a marketable star in the process, Bowie didn't stop wearing make-up. It had a transformative effect that was essential to his stagecraft, as important as the sound. And nothing was accidental. He knew exactly what effect he wanted to create – on everyone. It was always the shock of something new.

THE (HAIR) HALL-OF-FAME

Not all rock stars changed their hair as often as they changed their underwear. Mick Jagger has basically had the same cut since 1964. Others, meanwhile, did undergo a metamorphosis but are still known for one above all others. Freddie Mercury's pomaded crop complete with handlebar moustache springs to mind. Bowie's hair wasn't simply hair, however. It was part of his evolutionary process. His best styles were the ones that already had a kernel of popularity in the backstreets of cool. What Bowie did was to bring it into the mainstream by becoming its frontman and then, of course, abandoning it for something newer as soon as it reached the height of its popularity.

1971

Vital stats: Shoulder-length, slightly wavy and side-parted, Bowie's *Hunky Dory* look was dresses, suede boots and shaggy hair. It wasn't groomed, but free-flowing; the calm before the storm that was Ziggy Stardust.

1976

Vital stats: Ziggy's gravity-defying hair didn't happen by chance. Bowie wanted something drastic. Journalist Christopher Zara tells its origin story in *David Bowie: A Life*. Suzi Ronson was the woman responsible for the cut and colour that would influence an entire generation of rock fans, although it was based on a look of Kansai Yamamoto's. 'As Ronson tells it, Bowie was searching intently for something different, an entirely new look.' She didn't just fashion a look, however. She fashioned a look that needed a lot of work, therefore securing herself a full-time job on the road. As she told Zara, 'I wanted to be on the bus, not waving at it.' And it wasn't just red, but intoxicatingly red.

Vital stats: In the late seventies, Bowie sported a long crop that was slicked back as the Thin White Duke. It was dyed a combination of flame orange and platinum blonde. Needless to say, this could have looked disastrously DIY. Instead, it was severe and subversive.

19 83

Vital stats: By the time he sang *Let's Dance*, Bowie was two things he hadn't been in a long time: blond and bronzed. His peroxide curls were impressively robust, barely moving as he sang the opening, and at times during the tour, presumably as his hair grew while on the road, it almost looked like a pompadour.

Vital stats: Teddy Antolin was responsible for Bowie's hair on the Glass Spider Tour, which was classic rock 'n' roll. Longer and darker than on the later Serious Moonlight Tour, it possessed a swoon-worthy quality that paired brilliantly with leather jackets.

Vital stats: In the mid- to late-
nineties, Bowie was sporting a
goatee and short hair that stood
on end. He was wearing a lot of
Alexander McQueen, hence the
slightly punk hairstyle. At 1996's BRIT
Awards, Bowie was given an award
by Tony Blair. The Prime Minister
(at the time), was younger by six
years, but looked hopelessly square
next to Bowie, whose hair was spiked
upwards so that it almost looked
electrified.

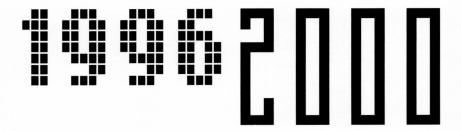

Vital stats: By the Millenium, Bowie
decided to resurrect a hairstyle that
he hadn't worn since the seventies.
His *Hunky Dory* waves were back
and totally befitting of his relaxed
rocker wardrobe of embroidered
coats and striped shirting.

FAKING

It's true that some of Bowie's make-up signatures aren't copyable outside of Halloween. They're simply too famous to be anything other than a cheap imitation. Bowie can't be reduced to painting by numbers, but that's not to say that several of his tricks can't be woven into your repertoire without arousing suspicion.

CHEEKS

As Aladdin Sane, Bowie's skin was flushed pink by make-up artist Pierre La Roche, as pretty as cotton candy. The lightning bolt always steals its thunder but while you can't walk around with zig-zag on your face (at least not every day), you can up the ante when it comes to your application of blusher. To achieve a similarly luminous sheen, opt for cream over powder, using the stick to draw an arc from your inner eye towards your temple in the shape of a 'C'. Quickly blend with your fingers then finish with a swipe of highlighter powder using a brush.

IT

EYESHADOW

As the Goblin King, Bowie wore a silvery eyeshadow from lash line to eyebrow, which created a surprisingly subtle effect compared to his 'villain' hair in 1986's Labyrinth, which was mastermind by the make-up artists Nick Dudman, Derry Haws and make-up supervisor Wally Schneiderman. Strangely enough, he did something similar for *Life on Mars?*, creating an electric blue ring around his eyes that was enhanced by the fact that he'd shaved off his brows at the time. In both cases, he wanted to pack a punch, letting his eyes become the focus. MAC's Dazzleshadow does exactly what it says on the tin for a stay-put spangle, and is available in more than 10 shades. Jareth would be tempted by 'It's All About Shine'.

EYELINER

In 1973, *Music Scene* published an article called, 'David Bowie's Makeup Dos and Don'ts,' which, presumably, would have stopped fans in their tracks. When it came to his eye make-up, it noted that among his 'basic essentials' was kohl, which he used for much of his career. More than two decades after the article was published, Bowie was still lining his eyes, which, combined with his short-back-and-sides cut, gave him an impish quality – an androgynous smoulder. Beauty experts rate Victoria Beckham's Satin Kajal Eyeliner, as well as Rimmel's Scandaleyes Waterproof Kohl Kajal.

LIPS

You don't often see a frosted lip out in the field these days, let alone metallic. Bowie wore both as Ziggy. Get the look without literally going for gold, silver or bronze by finding a richly-pigmented red that's cut with a shimmer of gold. Byredo's Liquid Lipstick Vinyl has a shade called 'Baiser Cosmique', which fits the bill. You can also try Maybelline's SuperStay Vinyl Ink Long-Lasting Liquid Lipstick. According to *Music Scene*, Bowie also relied on Elizabeth Arden's Eight Hour Cream, rubbing the formula onto his lips and eyes to make them look dewy.

NAILS

In *The Man Who Fell To Earth*, Bowie's character has white painted nails. For a man who was no stranger to manicures, it wasn't an obvious choice. He favoured electric blue, or glittery silver, as Ziggy, often just colouring the nail on his middle fingers, but I have to say, there's something about the neat white nails on Newton. It's stark but surprisingly chic. Just make sure to apply a few coats until it's even.

MEET YOUR (STYLE)

SOUL
MATE

'You would think that a rock star being married to a super-model would be one of the greatest things in the world. It is.'

DAVID BOWIE

They would have been the ultimate power couple in the early nineties, not least because of how good they looked together. Both had an ability to make what they were wearing, even if it was something as nondescript as a white muscle tee and a pair of high-waisted trousers, look deliciously cool. David and Iman, who met in 1990, were not just soulmates, but were cut from the same cloth when it came to style. He was the constantly reinventing rock star. She was the supermodel who was enough of a face to close fashion shows. (As Iman put it during a video interview with *Vogue*, 'At that time, I literally only wore Alaïa. [...] I think I seduced my husband in Alaïa. I went to lunch in Alaïa. I walked the streets in Alaïa.') And when they stepped out together, they had a chemistry that is still palpable in pictures (and must have been electrifying to witness in person).

Towards the end of 1990, the new couple attended a charity event in New York. In several photos, they're giggling together, both sets of elbows propped on a starched white tablecloth that's laid with wine glasses and a packet of Marlboros. She's wearing a scoop-necked lace minidress with sheer tights, inching a few centimetres above him thanks to a pair of pumps. He's wearing a tobacco-brown trouser suit, tailored to sit on the oversized side. Anyone present must have immediately known two things: they brought out the best in each other (as all great partners do) and they were meant to be together.

HOW TO BE THE BEST DRESSED COUPLE

Preternaturally good looks help, of course, but seriously, being the best dressed couple – whether the partnership is romantic or platonic – is more a state of mind. David and Iman, you can tell from the pictures, basked in each other's company. That was the real magic, and the clothes were just a bonus. Having said that, they did leave something of a blueprint for aspiring power couples to copy.

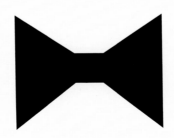

1

Wear Complementary Colours

Whether it was planned or not, the couple's outfits were often complementary without being matchy-matchy. In June 1991, they were photographed walking arm-in-arm through Paris. Iman looked very polished and very Parisian, dressed in a blue-and-white checked three-piece – leggings, a blazer and a flat cap. She was the picture of elegance, carrying a top-handle patent handbag and wearing bow-tied ballet pumps. Bowie's own blazer picked out the navy of the trench coat she wore over the top, although it was a slightly brighter shade, almost petrol.

Choosing a similar colour palette to whoever you happen to be going out with, whether it's a partner or a friend, might sound strangely calculated, but it's also strangely fun. You don't need to labour the point by wearing exactly the same shade from top-to-toe. It just needs to be an accent – a burgundy shoe for them, a slick of wine lip gloss for you – to make an impact.

Contrast

Having said that, you could also try another trick from the Bowie and Iman playbook. At 1999's MTV Awards, it's no exaggeration to say that they looked like they were going to completely different parties and had met, by chance, on the red carpet. Bowie looked like an off-duty rocker, wearing his long-sleeved top and parachute pants without an iota of showmanship. He had come as himself, the only concession to his status as a rock god being some little round sunglasses. Iman, on the other hand, was wearing a satin column dress, corseted and the colour of egg yolk, with a spangled handbag. The contrast was simply sublime.

Tailoring

Iman and Bowie both looked brilliant in tailoring, which has a strong association with the nineties. The decade when they met was much more minimal than the eighties – which was a time of decadence – and an unstudied elegance was the name of the game. For David and Iman, this meant separates that were more than the sum of their parts. Bowie would wear light beige tailoring, which sat loosely on his slight frame, with suede lace-ups and a white T-shirt. Iman wore a leather blazer and black leggings. They looked like a walking advert for Calvin Klein (and, in fact, Tommy Hilfiger, Bowie's friend and neighbour in Mustique, did eventually shoot them together for a 2003 campaign). You sadly can't buy that kind of charisma. What you can do, though, is comb through the menswear sections of second-hand shops for single-breasted blazers and pleat-front trousers, mixing and matching the resulting plunder with staples like a grey cashmere sweater or a white shirt from your existing wardrobe.

Be yourself

I highly suspect that by the time he met Iman, as he was entering his mid-forties, what to wear was even less of a big deal to Bowie. Over the next 10 years, almost whenever they appeared together at events in their adopted hometown of New York, he'd often step out in a simple trouser suit. Iman sometimes made more of a statement, like the time she paired a leopard-print corset with spike-toed court pumps, a similarly spotted handbag clutched in the hand that wasn't holding Bowie's. The lesson to learn is this: if you want to be the best-dressed couple of people in a room, whether you're romantically involved or not, the key is to be yourselves.

CONCLUSION

So there you have it: 10 style principles that will hopefully make the daily task of getting dressed slightly less humdrum, and slightly more thrilling. Bowie probably would have bristled at the idea of his wardrobe – his original, extraordinary and iconoclastic wardrobe – being categorised in such a way. So, perhaps, the ultimate takeaway is to trust your own instincts. Bowie didn't always get it right (that would hardly be the point), but he always had fun with fashion. And so can you.

PICTURE CREDITS

Images kindly provided by: Alamy (p. 114 Keystone Press); Getty
(p. 11 Gijsbert Hanekroot; p.23 Michael Ochs Archives; p.34 Lynn
Goldsmith; p.55 Michael Ochs archives; p. 58 Kevin.Mazur; p.67
Mark and Colleen Hayward; p.68 Michael Ochs Archives; p.69
Michael Ochs Archives; p.80 Steve Wood; p.94 Chris Walter; p.101
Michael Ochs Archives; p.107 Steve Schapiro; p.126 Mirrorpix;
p.137 LGI Stock; p.140 Michael Putland; p. 155 KMazur; p.160
Gijsbert Hanekroot; p.165 Michael Ochs Archives; p.169 KMazur;
p.176 Pool ARNAL/GARCIA; p.181 ARNAL/PAT); Unsplash (p. 102
Zoltan Tasi; p.109 Dwayne Joe; p.119 Clem Onojeghuo (top left),
Frank Flores (top right), Tyler Nix (bottom left), Troy Spoelma
(bottom right); p.149 Brian Lundquist (top left), Olha Ivanova (top
right), Joshua Rondeau (bottom left), Brian Asare (bottom right)).

REFERENCES

Bowie, David, 'Bowie in quotes: "I wouldn't like to make singing a full-time occupation".' *The Guardian* (11 Jan 2016). <https://www.theguardian.com/music/musicblog/2016/jan/11/david-bowie-life-in-quotes>

Bowie, David, *David Bowie: The Last Interview and Other Conversations* (Melville House Publishing, 2016)

'David Bowie's Makeup Dos and Don'ts.' *Music Scene* (November 1973). <https://www.bowiewonderworld.com/press/70/7311makeup.htm>

Evitts, Jared and Pigott, Paul, 'Harry Styles concert leaves "feather boa massacre" in Cardiff.' BBC (21 June 2023). <https://www.bbc.com/news/uk-wales-65971841>

Hagler, Tom, *Bowie at the BBC: A Life in Interviews* (Welbeck, 2023)

Horwell, Veronica, 'Kansai Yamamoto obituary.' *The Guardian* (28 July 2020). <https://www.theguardian.com/fashion/2020/jul/28/kansai-yamamoto-obituary>

'Iman Breaks Down 17 Looks From 1975 to Now | Life in Looks.' *Vogue* (2020). <https://www.youtube.com/watch?v=NmD_gxqD3hc>

'Inside Iman & David Bowie's Scenic Home Filled With Wonderful Objects.' *Vogue* (2022). <https://www.youtube.com/watch?v=fk9cq3gRCP0>

Jones, Dylan, *David Bowie: A Life* (Windmill Books, 2018)

Sheffield, Rob, *On Bowie* (Headline, 2016)

Skidmore, Maisie, 'Flash of Genius: Photographing Aladdin Sane.' *AnOther* (23 December 2015). < https://www.anothermag.com/art-photography/8162/flash-of-genius-photographing-aladdin-sane?>

Soligny, Jérôme, *David Bowie Rainbowman: 1967–1980* (Monoray, 2023)

Thomas, Dana, 'David Bowie, Alexander McQueen, and the Making of That Iconic 90s-Era Union Jack Coat.' *Vanity Fair* (11 January 2016). <https://www.vanityfair.com/style/2016/01/david-bowie-alexander-mcqueen-era-union-jack-coat>

Victoria and Albert Museum, 'Fashion in Motion: Kansai Yamamoto.' V&A website. <https://www.vam.ac.uk/articles/fashion-in-motion-kansai-yamamoto>

White, Ben, 'David Bowie & Mos Def: The Style Council (2003 Cover Story).' *Complex* (August/September 2003). <https://www.complex.com/music/a/ben-white/david-bowie-mos-def-2003-cover-story>

Display quote sources

Introduction
David Bowie interviewed on BBC Radio, 8 January 1997. Quoted in *Bowie at the BBC: A Life in Interviews*, by Tom Hagler (Welbeck, 2023)

Chapter 1
Woody Woodmansey. Quoted in *Bowie at the BBC: A Life in Interviews*, by Tom Hagler (Welbeck, 2023)

Chapter 2
David Bowie interviewed for *Rolling Stone*, 23 April 1987. Quoted in *David Bowie: The Last Interview and Other Conversations* (Melville House Publishing, 2016)

Chapter 3
Dana Gillespie. Quoted in *David Bowie Rainbowman: 1967–1980*, by Jérôme Soligny (Monoray, 2023)

Chapter 4
Terry O'Neill interviewed for *The Guardian*, 6 August 2019. Quoted in *The Guardian*, 'Terry O'Neill on his best Bowie shoots: "David never needed coaxing",' by Thomas Hobbs. <https://www. theguardian.com/artanddesign/2019/ aug/06/terry-oneill-best-bowie-shoots- david-never-needed-coaxing>

Chapter 5
Eddie Clarke. Quoted in *David Bowie Rainbowman: 1967–1980*, by Jérôme Soligny (Monoray, 2023)

Chapter 6
David Bowie interviewed for *Vox Pop*, 18 March 1987. Quoted in *David Bowie: The Last Interview and Other Conversations* (Melville House Publishing, 2016)

Chapter 7
David Bowie interviewed for *Bust* magazine, 2000. Quoted in *David Bowie: The Last Interview and Other Conversations* (Melville House Publishing, 2016)

Chapter 8
David Bowie interviewed for *Esquire*, March 2004. Quoted in *Esquire*, 'David Bowie: What I've learned. Sage wisdom from a one-of-a-kind artist.' <https://www. esquire.com/entertainment/music/news/ a41108/david-bowie-what-ive-learned/>

Chapter 9
David Bowie, quoting John Lennon, in an interview with *Vox Pop*, 18 March 1987. Quoted in *David Bowie: The Last Interview and Other Conversations* (Melville House Publishing, 2016)

Chapter 10
David Bowie. Quoted on *Goodreads*. <https://www.goodreads.com/author/ quotes/10360.David_Bowie?page=1>

ACKNOWLEDGEMENTS

Thank you to my wonderful editing team at Ebury – Sam and Lucie – for their unfailing support, as well as copy-editor extraordinaire Kate, whose thoughtful precision made this a much better book. Thank you also to the designer, Claire Rochford, and illustrator, Ollie Mann. You both brought these pages to life.

To my dear friend Hannah, who was kind enough to drop this opportunity into my lap in the first place. Thank you for your generosity.

To Rachael, Caspar and Juno, who offered me so much encouragement about this project – and who even took me on a walking tour of Montreux.

To my family – my parents, Amy and Richard, my brother-in-law, Johnny, and my darling nephew, Xan, who already sings his own rendition of Rebel Rebel. Your constant love keeps me going.

And finally, to my sister, Emma. As little girls, one of us was always reading, writing and imagining. I will never stop being grateful to have grown up next to your brilliant mind and to have stolen your interests as my own. Thank you for leading the way and never leaving my side.

ABOUT THE AUTHOR

Natalie Hammond is the senior fashion news editor at
Grazia. She previously worked on the fashion desk at
The Times, and her writing has appeared in publications
including *The Telegraph*, *The Financial Times* and
gal-dem. She studied English Literature at the University
of Exeter, and has a master's degree in Magazine
Journalism from City University. This is her first book.

1

Published in 2024 by Pop Press, an imprint of Ebury Publishing,
20 Vauxhall Bridge Road,
London SW1V 2SA

Pop Press is part of the Penguin Random House group of companies
whose addresses can be found at global.penguinrandomhouse.com

First published by Pop Press in 2024

www.penguin.co.uk

A CIP catalogue record for this book is available
from the British Library

ISBN 9781529932881

Text by Natalie Hammond
Design by: Claire Rochford
Illustrations by: Ollie Mann
Photography: Getty images, except pages 102, 109, 119, 149 Unsplash
and page 144 Alamy.
Printed and bound in Malaysia by Times Offset (M) Sdn Bhd